SCHIRMER PERFORMANCE EDITIONS

THE CLASSICAL ERA
Early Intermediate Level

Compiled and Edited by Richard Walters

AUDIO ACCESS INCLUDED
Recorded Performances Online

Recorded by

Elena Abend
Matthew Edwards
Stefanie Jacob
Jennifer Linn

To access companion recorded performances online, visit:
www.halleonard.com/mylibrary

Enter Code
3334-5616-0375-4615

On the cover:
Blind Man's Bluff (1789)
by Francisco de Goya (1746–1828)

ISBN 978-1-4803-3822-7

G. SCHIRMER, *Inc.*

DISTRIBUTED BY

HAL•LEONARD®
CORPORATION
7777 W. BLUEMOUND RD. P.O. BOX 13819 MILWAUKEE, WI 53213

www.musicsalesclassical.com
www.halleonard.com

T0050640

CONTENTS

Though the table of contents appears in alphabetical order by composer, the music in this book is in progressive order.

The price of this publication includes access to companion recorded performances online, for download or streaming, using the unique code found on the title page. Visit **www.halleonard.com/mylibrary** and enter the access code.

The music in this collection has been edited by the compiler/editor Richard Walters, except for the pieces previously published in other volumes in the Schirmer Performance Editions series:

Beethoven: German Dance; Ecossaise; Sonatina
from *Beethoven: Selected Piano Works*
edited and recorded by Matthew Edwards

Clementi: Sonatina
from *Clementi: Sonatinas, Opus 36*
edited and recorded by Jennifer Linn

Mozart: Allegro in F Major; Minuet in G Major; Minuet in F Major; Allegro in B-flat Major
from *Mozart: 15 Easy Piano Pieces*
edited and recorded by Elena Abend

COMPOSER BIOGRAPHIES
AND
PERFORMANCE NOTES

It is likely that the commentary below will not be read through as a whole, but only in reference to a specific composer or piece. Therefore, many ideas stated regarding Classical Era style are repeated many times.

A few general comments about Classical Era style:

- Music of the Classical period will risk sounding dull if the musician does not apply insightful articulation, which alongside clarity and steadiness, is an essential component of Classical style.

- The default touch is *portato*, playing notes without indication of articulation with a slight separation.

- Legato touch generally should only be applied to notes marked with a slur.

- Articulation is part of the music and should be learned along with notes and rhythms from the beginning of practice.

- The sustaining pedal should generally not be used.

- Classical Era music is excellent for developing a refined tone and touch.

LUDWIG VAN BEETHOVEN
German composer and pianist.
Born in Bonn, December 16, 1770;
died in Vienna, March 28, 1827.

Beethoven was the major figure of the transition from the Classical Era to the Romantic Era in music. As one of the first successful freelance composers, as opposed to a composer thriving in a royal court appointment, Beethoven wrote widely in nearly every genre of his day, with emphasis on instrumental music. He acquired wealth and fame beyond any composer before him. Beethoven's chamber music, piano sonatas, concertos and symphonies are part of the ever present international repertoire. In his youth he was regarded as one of the greatest pianists of his time, but he stopped performing after hearing loss set in. He devoted an enormous amount of his compositional efforts to the piano, which as an instrument came of age during his lifetime. He was occasionally a piano teacher, with wealthy patrons and young prodigies begging for lessons, though this task was not a match for his nature. However, teaching piano did inspire him to write many pieces for students. Because his piano music is so widely spread across the level of difficulty from easy to virtuoso, Beethoven's piano music is played by students and professional pianists.

German Dance in C Major, WoO 8, No. 1
This simple, song-like piece has the flavor of a German folk dance. This is clearly not a waltz. It is more akin to a ländler. The melody is in the right hand and the left hand plays an accompaniment. The right hand articulation is independent of that of the left hand. The left hand accompaniment figure in measures 1–7 and 13–15 might be approached in two different ways: one would be a light separation between each note of the figure; a second approach, also defendable, would be to slur beat 1 to beat 2, with separation on beat 3. Either approach works. Experiment and find which you prefer. Tempo is an interpretive choice. One can imagine a tempo at a slower pace than on the companion recorded performance. We advise no pedal in practicing or performing this piece.

Ecossaise in E-flat Major, WoO 86
An ecossaise is a dance with French origins that became popular in Vienna during Beethoven's time. This is a breezy, happy piece. Part of the fun of the music is the bounce of the repeated notes in the opening phrase. The B section that begins in measure 10 develops rhythmic and melodic aspects of the last measures of the A section. Notice that in Classical Era articulation it is common to have a two-note slur followed by two staccato notes. Tempo is up for interpretation

since Beethoven gave no indication. An acceptable range of tempos would be from that of the companion recording to slightly faster. One could play this piece with no pedal; another approach would be to pedal for one beat only on every downbeat, lifting the pedal on beat 2.

Sonatina in G Major, Anh. 5, No. 1 (attributed to Beethoven)

The authorship of this sonatina is questionable. Scholars now believe it likely that it is not by Beethoven. The sonatina falls easily under the hands, and when played with insight is a sparkling gem. Music of the Classical period will sound dull and uninteresting if the musician does not apply insightful articulation, which alongside clarity and steadiness, is an essential component of Classical style.

Notice that the composer generally asks us to play quietly in the first movement, Moderato. This requires a refined, gentle touch. A key component of Classical style at the keyboard is an accompaniment figure called the Alberti Bass, such as in the left hand in measures 5–6 and 21–22. To master Classical style, you must master the Alberti Bass. It requires smoothness and quietness. Generally you should think of slurring each pattern; in this case, covering two beats. Slurring simply means to play the notes within the slur as *legato*. A slur is not the same as a phrase, which is a longer musical statement. You might try a very slight lift after beat one of measure 5 in the left hand to mark the beginning of a new slur on beat 3. The distinction between the slurred figures of this accompaniment figure should be extremely subtle. The composer has provided a few clues about articulation, and we have added other editorial suggestions appropriate to this style. You can also hear these details of articulation on the companion recorded performance. An excellent idea from the recorded pianist is to change the articulation on the repeat of the section that begins in measure 9. An interpretive option would be play the eighth notes from beats 2 to 4 in measures 10, 12, 13, and 14 as slurred notes the first time through and as gentle staccato on the repeat. Many could debate whether pedal is appropriate in this style, but almost no one would dispute the fact that any pedaling should be extremely light and inconspicuous. We recommend no use of pedal in this sonatina, instead relying on all aspects of articulation to be clearly from the fingers only. Note that the articulation is not always the same in both hands,

such as in measure 8. The form is rather like an abbreviated Rondo, with measures 1–8 as a theme which returns in measure 17. Measures 9–16 are a contrasting B section. The composer creates new material for the ending of the final section, beginning in measure 25. The pianist on the recording offers an interesting interpretation option in measure 16, with a slight *rit.* heading back into the material from the beginning.

The texture throughout the Romanza movement is a single-note melody in the right hand and accompaniment figures in the left hand. The composer indicates eighth notes for all the notes in measure 1; a similar pattern is found in measures 3 and 4, but he asks us to hold the lowest note. This movement is a "Romanza," which is indication of a song-like spirit and form. It has a simple form of ABA plus Coda. An interesting interpretive idea from the pianist on the companion recording is to make the fermata longer in measure 19 on the repeat. Note that in this Classical style, the grace notes in measures 30 and 34 begin on the beat. Articulation needs to be clean; it would be best to play this movement without pedal to emphasize clarity. We have added stylistic editorial suggestions of articulation in brackets. If you play all the notes of the piece the same, with no attention to articulation, phrase, or style, your result will be very boring. One hint in Classical style in playing short slurs is to make a slight lift before moving on to the next slur. For instance: in measure 2 in the right hand, a very slight lift after the G before attacking the next slur beginning on B. This lift must be very subtle and cannot be overstated, and the music must remain in tempo.

GEORG ANTONIN BENDA
Bohemian violinist and composer.
Born in Staré Benátky, June 30, 1722; died in Köstritz, November 6, 1795.

Benda immigrated to Prussia from his native Bohemia, first working as a court violinist and then as Kapellmeister to Duke Friedrich III of Saxe-Gotha. Benda was successful in introducing opera to the court, a genre held in suspicion by many of the pious leaders in the community. The composer began writing for a theatre group in 1774, combining opera and theatre traditions into what came to be termed melodrama. After some time in Hamburg and Vienna, Benda retired outside Gotha, where he continued to compose, conduct, and perform until his death. Remembered today as a composer of German melodramas, Benda was equally famous during his life for his church music and a small collection of piano sonatas and sonatinas.

Sonatina No. 10 in F Major

This is an example of *stile galante*, an early classical style from the mid-eighteenth century. *Stile galante* was a deliberate change in aesthetic from the thick counterpoint of the high Baroque. This music is both graceful and lively. Like any music of this period, stylistic details are accomplished through articulation. This simple piece is full of variety. In your careful preparation, the articulation of each figure, and the elegant moving from figure to figure, will create an enchanting performance. Notice details such as in measure 2 in the left hand, staccato on the second half of beat 1, and slurred eighth notes on beats 2 and 3. Also, in the right hand, in the first measure, notice three slurred triplets followed by three smoothly played quarter-note chords. The sixteenth notes in measures 5 and 6 and in other similar places alternate between the hands, which is fun to play. Listen very carefully to your playing so that these sixteenth notes are all exactly even rhythmically and dynamically. This scurrying motion is followed by smoothly played eighth notes in measure 7. The form is ABA, with the B section beginning in measure 16. A sonatina is an abbreviated sonata form. Sonata form was still being developed in this period. One could view measures 29–32 as a brief development section. Remember that Benda wrote in a period when there was no sustaining pedal on the instrument. We recommend that you play with no pedal. Take care that you do not speed up in the sections of moving sixteenth notes.

MUZIO CLEMENTI

Italian composer, pianist, teacher, publisher, and piano manufacturer.
Born in Rome, January 23, 1752;
died in Evesham, March 10, 1832.

By age 13 Clementi was organist at San Lorenzo in Rome. Peter Beckford heard the youth and brought him to study at his English estate for the next seven years. Clementi then moved to London, where performing and publishing propelled him to embark on a series of concert tours from 1780–1785. During one of these tours he entered a duel with Mozart, determining who was the better keyboard player, an evening's amusement organized by Emperor Joseph II. The contest was declared a tie. Clementi acquired many famous piano students all over Europe during his travels, including Carl Czerny, John Field, and Frédéric Chopin. Returning to London in 1785, he continued to teach some of the wealthiest and most-talented pianists of his day, and amassed enough capital to invest in music publishing and piano manufacturing. In 1802 he began another European tour, not only concertizing, but promoting his pianos and signing composers to his publishing company, including the young Beethoven. From 1810 until his death, Clementi ran his publishing company and piano manufacturing company, and made some unsuccessful attempts at symphonic writing. His piano sonatas and sonatinas (written for his piano students) were his most popular compositions during his life and remained so after his death.

Sonatina in C Major, Op. 36, No. 1

This is perhaps the most famous of all sonatinas for piano and has been played by countless students for the last two hundred years. A sonatina is an abbreviated sonata form.

The first movement, Allegro, is unusual in its form. It begins like a normal sonatina, with an exposition that goes through measure 15, followed by a brief development section in measures 16–23. But in the return to the opening material Clementi surprises us by moving an octave lower. Then after four measures, he abandons the first theme and creates something new to the end. This music needs crisp clarity. As you would with almost any piece, practice first at a slow tempo. Also, at this early state of practice you should not only be learning the notes, but also articulation and dynamics, which are an organic part of music, not details to be sprinkled on at the last stages of preparing a piece for performance. Carefully observe where there is a slur, and which notes are to be played short, without slurring. Notes that are unmarked in articulation only occur in the left hand in this piece. The quarter notes that begin in the end of measure 6 and continue through measure 8 should be played with slight separation. The same is true for the left hand quarter notes in measures 20–21. The eighth-note Alberti Bass figure in measures 9, 11, 32, and 34 should be played quietly and smoothly. No pedal should be used in this piece. It is very important to maintain a steady tempo throughout.

Like much piano music of the Classical period, the second movement (Andante) uses an accompanying figure in the left hand. The triplets in measures 1–3 and elsewhere in the piece need to be played smoothly, quietly, and evenly. You should practice this accompaniment figure alone, without the melody. The trills (such as in measures 3, 21, and 25) begin on the beat, not before it, and on the note above in this period, with an escape at the end of the trill. An escape is the two small notes that are played just before moving to the next principal note. Be careful to notice details in this composition such as dynamics, which vary a great deal, and the composer's marked slurs (which indicate that the small group of slurred notes should be played legato). Beware not to take this andante too quickly.

The happy third movement (Vivace) should be played with crisp articulation, careful attention to dynamics, and a tempo that is lively but not out of control. Some students attempt to play this movement more quickly than they can master. There is also a tendency among some pianists to rush forward in this music. Be sure to keep a steady beat throughout. The left hand accompaniment figure needs to be quiet and smooth, without calling undue attention to itself.

CARL CZERNY

Austrian teacher, pianist, composer, theorist, and historian.
Born in Vienna, February 21, 1791;
died in Vienna, July 15, 1857.

Czerny began playing the piano at the age of three and was composing by the age of seven. His father was a piano teacher and supervised much of the boy's education until Czerny became one of Beethoven's students. From 1805 onward, Czerny dedicated much of his time to teaching, acquiring many famous students, including Liszt, Thalberg, and Leschetizky. Czerny often composed pieces for his students as an aid in developing a specific technical skill. In addition to his numerous pedagogical piano studies, for which he is best-remembered today, Czerny published hundreds of other works, including symphonies, variations, arrangements, chamber music, and sacred choral pieces.

Study in C Major
from *100 Progressive Studies,* Op. 139, No. 10
Czerny's study is primarily about the repeated left hand notes. How do you quickly repeat the chords in the left hand without your hand and wrist becoming a tense claw? This requires help from you teacher, who can see your hand and advise you, but in general, approach the repeated chords with a loose wrist and feel a light bounce as you play them. It will help greatly to practice this slowly before attempting to play the repeated chords at tempo. Some teachers may advise you to alternate fingers on the repeated single notes, such as in measures 17–20. Another very important musical challenge in playing fast repeated notes and chords is to keep the tempo absolutely steady. Guard against the tendency to press the tempo and speed up in playing this kind of left hand figure. After all, the melody in the right hand is the principal attraction. The right hand articulation is completely separate from that of the left hand. Think of the right hand as smoothly sailing over the busy accompaniment. This is happy music and you should find the smile inside you while you play it.

Study in C Major
from *The Little Pianist,* Op. 823, No. 31
Here is a piece that shows how well you have mastered playing scales. Can you play a scale evenly? This piece will show whether you can or not, especially in measures 25–28. The entire piece is essentially a showcase for brief sections of scale work, spelled by slower moving rhythms. Articulation is what will make this short study interesting. We have made editorial suggestions for articulation that should help you bring this music to life. This piece should be played with restraint, gracefulness and refinement. It is very important that you keep a steady tempo throughout. Do not make the common mistake of either speeding up or slowing down in measures 25–28.

FRANZ JOSEPH HAYDN

Austrian composer.
Born in Rohrau, March 31, 1732;
died in Vienna, May 31, 1809.

One of the major composers of the eighteenth century, Haydn defined the sound of the Classical style. He was employed by the Esterházy court for the majority of his career, serving two Princes from the Hungarian ruling family in Vienna as well as Hungary. Later in his life, Haydn spent time in London composing for the German violinist and musical impresario Johann Peter Salomon (1745–1815). Haydn lived his last years in Vienna. He wrote in nearly every genre of his day including, most famously, operas, symphonies, and chamber music. Though his keyboard music is not as well-known as his orchestral works, he wrote over 50 piano sonatas and a large assortment of other keyboard pieces. Haydn's influence in Classical Era music is captured in the pet name by which he became known in his later life, "Papa Haydn," a term of endearment bestowed upon him by the hundreds of musicians who had learned from him. The nickname also refers to Haydn being the compositional father of the modern symphony.

Arietta
from *Variations in E-flat Major*, Hob. XVII/3

An arietta is a brief aria for a singer. This short piece is melodically driven, with the melody in the top note of the right hand. It has a sweet nature and Haydn has indicated as such with his marking of *dolce*. There are some rich harmonic changes, such as in measures 4–7. The slurred staccatos marked in measure 2 are probably the key to the piece. What does slurred staccato mean? Play the repeated notes with a sense of phrase, moving from the first to the last, but with slight separation. One would likely want to use pedal in a performance of this arietta, but practice should be done without pedal in the early stages. Pedaling should be added very discreetly and very carefully. Listen carefully to what the pedaling you choose does to the clarity of the notes. Above all, this is earnest music that needs to be played with sensitivity and simplicity.

Country Dance in C Major

Even master composers such as the great Haydn wrote teaching pieces like this simple country dance, which has a folk flavor about it. This dance in three is certainly not a waltz, but something more deliberate on each beat, such as a ländler. Even though this music is quite simple, there is still plenty of Classical Era style possible in a performance. Haydn gave us no markings about articulation in this piece. We have editorially suggested articulation in period style. Do not use pedal. Haydn is known for surprises as a composer, and the sudden triplet figure in measure 10 is certainly a surprise. Make sure in your performance that this sounds like a fun diversion in the texture, not a moment of panic. Be sure to keep a very steady beat throughout. Even though this is a country dance, this little composition asks you to play with taste and refinement.

WOLFGANG AMADEUS MOZART
Austrian composer.
Born in Salzburg, January 27, 1756;
died in Vienna, December 5, 1791.

One of the greatest talents in the history of music, Mozart was first a child prodigy as a composer, keyboard player and violinist. He developed into a composer unrivalled by any, with a vast output in opera, symphonies, choral music, keyboard music and chamber music, all accomplished before his death at the young age of 35. Mozart spent most of his adult life living and working in Vienna. He was at the end of the era when successful musicians and composers attained substantial royal court appointments. A major position of this sort eluded him, despite his enormous talent, and he constantly sought opportunities to compose and perform. His music embodies the eighteenth century "age of reason" in its refined qualities, but adds playfulness, earnestness, sophistication and a deep sense of melody and harmony. Mozart's piano sonatas, concertos, sets of variations, and many other pieces at all levels, from quite easy to virtuoso, are standards in the literature, played by pianists all over the world. His first compositions as a boy, from age 5, were for keyboard.

Allegro in F Major, KV 1c

A march-like quality pervades this piece, dated by Leopold Mozart as being written on December 11, 1761 in Salzburg, when Mozart was just five years old. It's easy to imagine the boy Wolfgang playing soldier in this music. It is in ABA form and is written in two voices throughout. Notice the editorial suggestion of echoing (*subito p* at the end of measure 6, followed by a *subito mf* at the end of measure 8) to bring interest to the repetitions of the melodic material. You can work on independence of the hands as well, carefully observing the right hand slurs against the staccato accompaniment in the left hand. Editorial suggestions of articulation (indicated in brackets) will help find the period style. Notice which notes are to be played staccato, and which are to be played as grouped in short slurs. We strongly recommend that this piece should be played without pedal.

Minuet in G Major, KV 1e/1f

The trio originated in the Baroque period as a contrast to the minuet. It was often performed by three players (hence, the labeling of "trio"). This minuet and trio were likely composed in late 1761 or early 1762 in Salzburg, around the time of Wolfgang's sixth birthday. Both the minuet and trio are written in ABA form with repeats. Graceful articulation in the appropriate style is shown in the editorial suggestions (in brackets). After playing the Trio, in the return to the Minuet do not play the repeats. Do not use pedaling in practicing or performing this piece.

Minuet in F Major, KV 2

This minuet was written during January 1762 in Salzburg, around the time of Mozart's sixth birthday. The form is ABA with repeats. The opening A section returns at measure 18 in a slightly modified version. This is a tightly knit composition, with the opening rhythmic motive, which is stated in the first measure and appears in all but six measures. Observe carefully the suggested articulations, particularly the staccato notes on beats two and three. This will give the minuet a graceful, dance-like quality. Use no pedal in practice or performance of this piece.

Allegro in B-flat Major, KV 3

This little piece is dated March 1762, written in Salzburg when Mozart was six years old. The form is ABA[1]. The piece is almost entirely written in only two voices, with a third voice added only to reinforce the tonic chord in measures 4, 6, 24, and 26. There are many editorial suggestions regarding articulation, which will help find the appropriate style. Avoid playing music of this period with a generally applied bland legato touch, which is not stylistically appropriate. Note which notes are staccato, and which are grouped in slurs. Practice and perform this piece with no pedal. Notice a suggested *decrescendo* and *ritardando* in measures 27 and 28 on the second time only, followed by a recommended **mf** *a tempo*.

IGNACE JOSEPH PLEYEL

Austrian composer, publisher, and piano maker.
Born in Ruppersthal, June 18, 1757;
died in Paris, November 14, 1831.

Pleyel was a student of Joseph Haydn, lodging at the Esterházy palace, where Haydn lived and worked, along with several other pupils under the patronage of Count Ladislaus Erdődy. After a visit to Italy, Pleyel served as assistant Kapellmeister and eventual Kappellmeister at Strasbourg Cathedral in France. The French Revolution forced him to move to London after all musical functions in Strasbourg stopped. Pleyel amassed a considerable fortune in London

organizing and performing in a concert series conceived by the impresario Wilhelm Cramer. After moving back to France he purchased a large Château which attracted the attention of many revolutionaries who were suspicious of any conspicuous display of wealth. Pleyel was imprisoned for aristocratic sympathies and was under the likely threat of death, but the composition of a patriotic hymn secured his freedom from incarceration and suspicion. In 1795, he moved to Paris and opened a publishing house, representing works by composers such as Boccherini, Beethoven, Clementi, Cramer, Dussek, Haydn, and even invented the concept of the miniature study score. Pleyel's publishing house folded soon after his death.

Sonatina No. 3 in F Major

Like all the pieces in this collection, Pleyel's sonatina requires careful attention to clarity. Classical style is all about clarity, articulation and steadiness. One should play this piece with no pedal. Any pedal would blur the fine details of the music. This music also requires absolute steadiness. The pianist on the companion recording has created a slight feeling of hesitation before moving into the repeat of the opening material. This good and graceful idea is the only acceptable deviation in an otherwise steady tempo. The left hand is a supportive accompaniment, the major exception happening in measures 21–22 when it takes over the principal melody. Pay very close attention to which notes should be staccato and which notes should be slurred (meaning that the small group of notes within the slur are played *legato*). In measures 13–18 appoggiaturas appear on beats 1 and 3. In this period appoggiaturas are played on the beat. The end result sounds rhythmically the same as four sixteenth notes. The *marcato* markings, such as in measure 3, are to be played especially crisp and short. They are also accented. You will have a colorful and lively result if you work at informing your performance with careful observation to articulation.

DANIEL GOTTLOB TÜRK

German theorist and composer.
Born in Claussnitz, August 10, 1750;
died in Halle, August 26, 1813.

Educated first by his musical father and then at the University of Leipzig, Türk studied with several of Bach's students and finally decided on a career in music. In 1774 he became the Kantor at the Ulrichskirche in Halle, and later the director of music at Halle University, as well as the music director at the Marktkirche. Beyond his teaching and church responsibilities he completed and published several books on the practicalities of being a church organist, improving church music, a textbook on keyboard playing, and various other theoretical and scientific works related to music. Though remembered today as a writer and advocate of music, he composed a notable output of works, of which several short keyboard pieces are still played.

Little Rondo
A rondo is distinguished by a returning theme. In this case, the theme only returns once, thus Türk's title "Little Rondo." The left hand eighth notes in measures 1–6 and 9–14 are quiet accompaniment to the right hand melody and should be played smoothly. The trills in measures 17 and 21 begin on the note above the principal note in this period. This piece should be played with no pedal. Your aim is clarity and steadiness. Note the suggested articulation in the right hand in measures 7–8 and 15.

—Richard Walters, editor
Joshua Parman, assistant editor

German Dance in C Major

Ludwig van Beethoven
WoO 8, No. 1

Edited and with fingering by Matthew Edwards.
Editorial suggestions are in brackets.

Minuet in F Major

Wolfgang Amadeus Mozart
KV 2

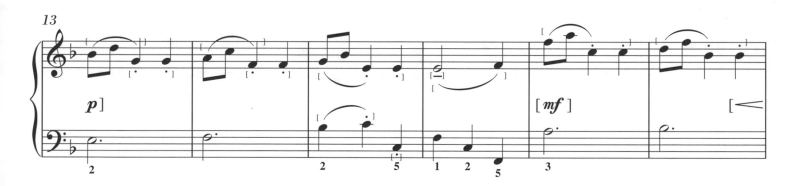

Edited and with fingering by Elena Abend.
Editorial suggestions are in brackets.

Allegro in F Major

Wolfgang Amadeus Mozart
KV 1c

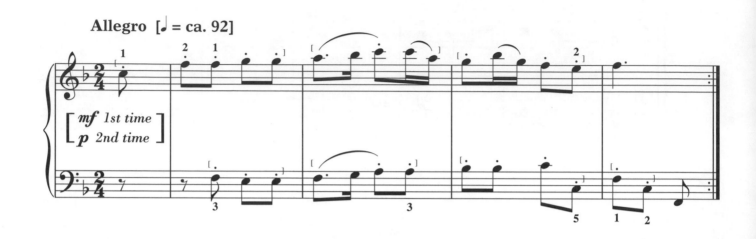

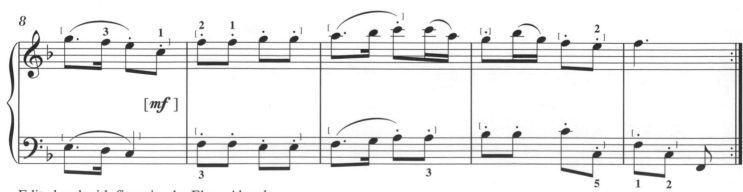

Edited and with fingering by Elena Abend.
Editorial suggestions are in brackets.

Allegro in B-flat Major

Wolfgang Amadeus Mozart
KV 3

Edited and with fingering by Elena Abend.
Editorial suggestions are in brackets.

Country Dance in C Major

Franz Joseph Haydn

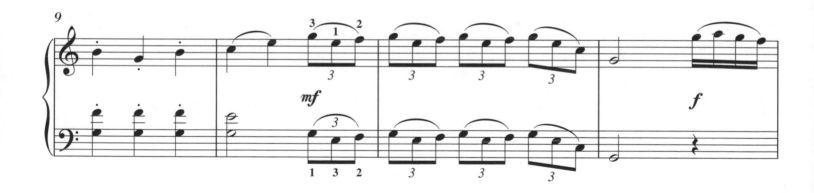

Fingering by Elena Abend.
Dynamics and articulations are stylistic editorial suggestions.

Little Rondo

Daniel Gottlob Türk

Fingering by Elena Abend.
Editorial suggestions are in brackets.

Study in C Major

from *The Little Pianist*

Carl Czerny
Op. 823, No. 31

Fingering by Stefanie Jacob.
Editorial suggestions are in brackets.

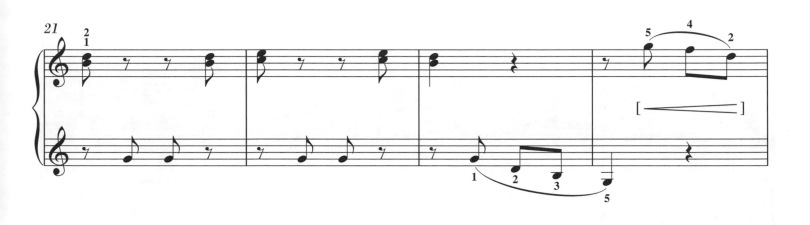

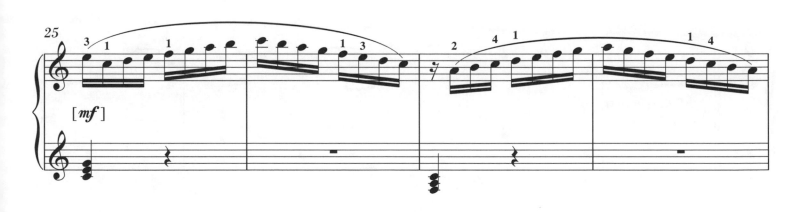

Minuet in G Major

Wolfgang Amadeus Mozart
KV le/lf

Eliminate repeats on the Da Capo.
Edited and with fingering by Elena Abend.
Editorial suggestions are in brackets.

Trio

**D.C. al Fine
second time**

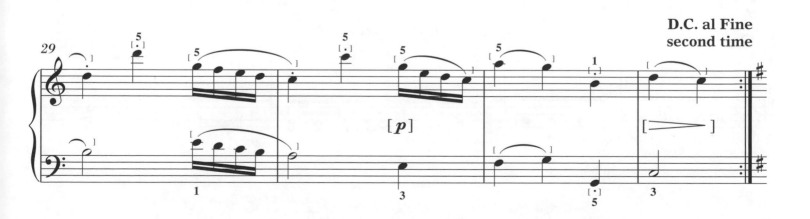

Study in C Major

from *100 Progressive Studies*

Carl Czerny
Op. 139, No. 10

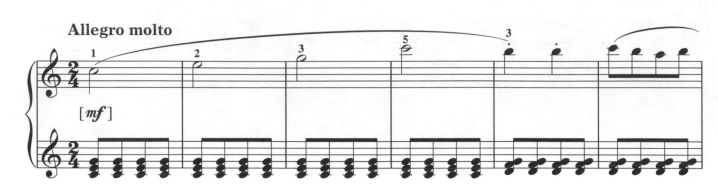

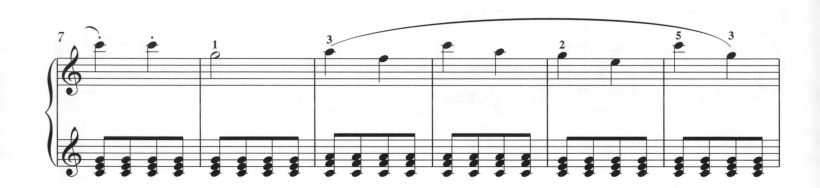

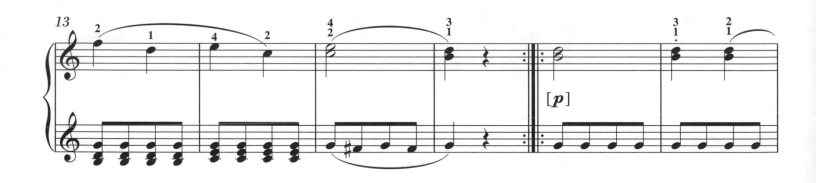

Fingering by Stefanie Jacob.
Editorial suggestions are in brackets.

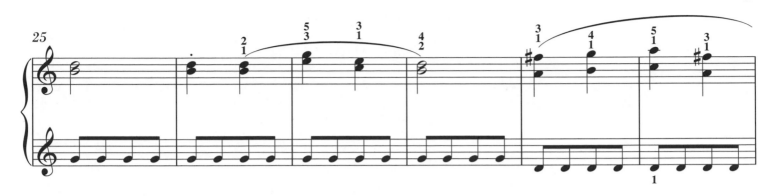

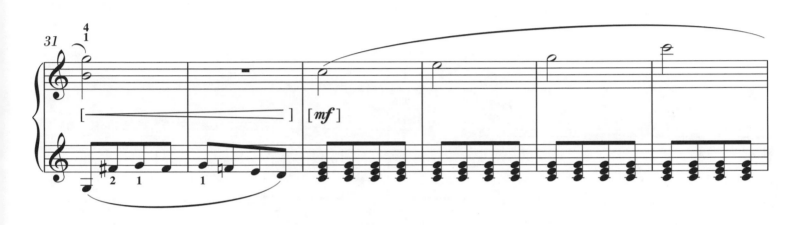

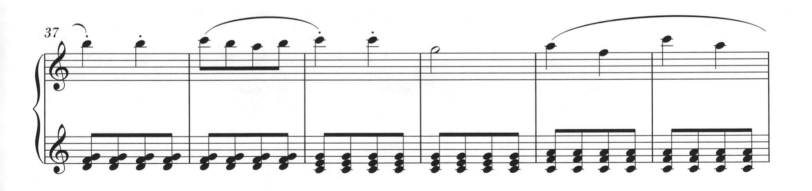

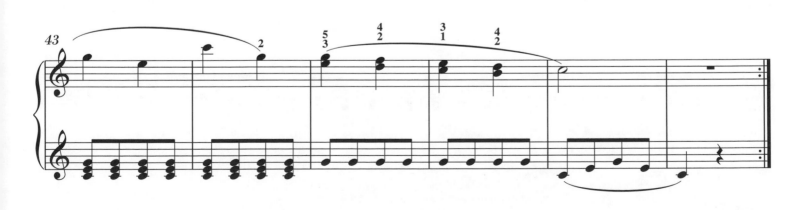

Ecossaise in E-flat Major

Ludwig van Beethoven
WoO 86

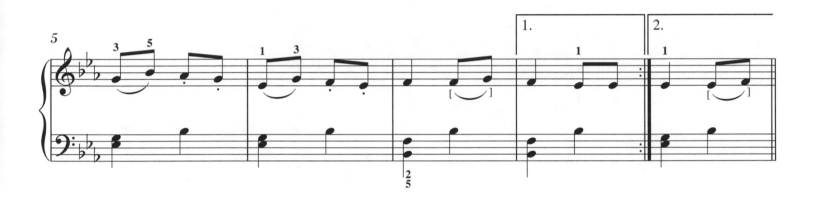

Edited and with fingering by Matthew Edwards.
Editorial suggestions are in brackets.

Sonatina No. 3 in F Major

Ignace Joseph Pleyel

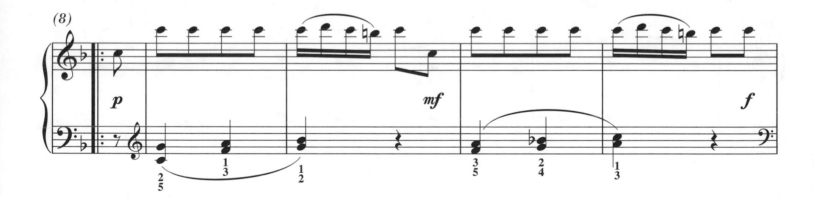

Fingering by Elena Abend.

Arietta
from *Variations in E-flat Major*

Franz Joseph Haydn
Hob. XVII/3

Fingering by Elena Abend.

Sonatina in G Major
I

Ludwig van Beethoven
Kinsky-Halm Anh. 5, No. 1

Edited and with fingering by Matthew Edwards.
Editorial suggestions are in brackets.

II

Romanza

Sonatina No. 10 in F Major

Georg Antonin Benda

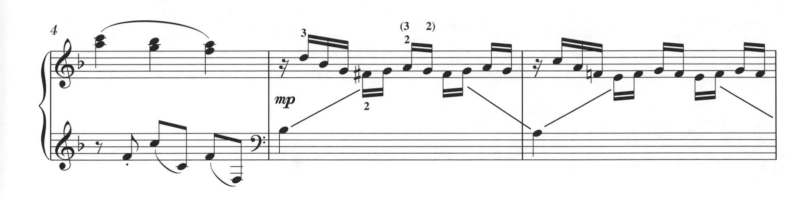

Fingering by Matthew Edwards.
Dynamics, articulations, and tempo are stylistic editorial suggestions.

Sonatina in C Major

I

Muzio Clementi
Op. 36, No. 1

Allegro [♩ = 80–100]

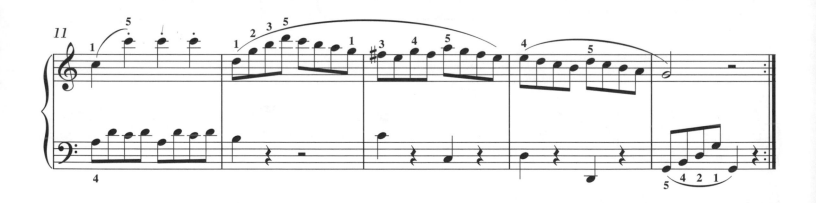

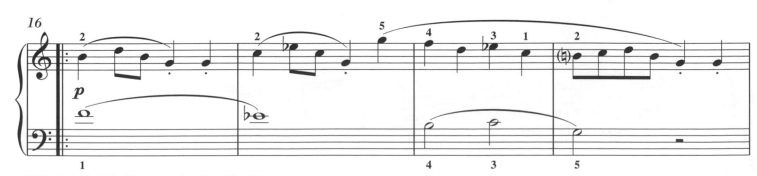

Edited and with fingering by Jennifer Linn.

*This repeat is omitted in the companion recording.

II

*optional

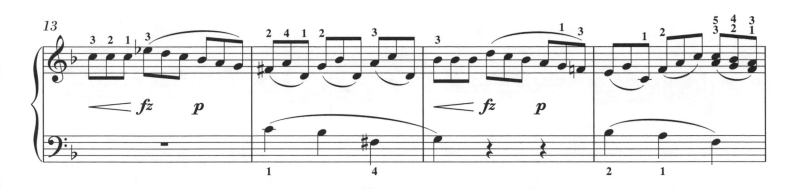

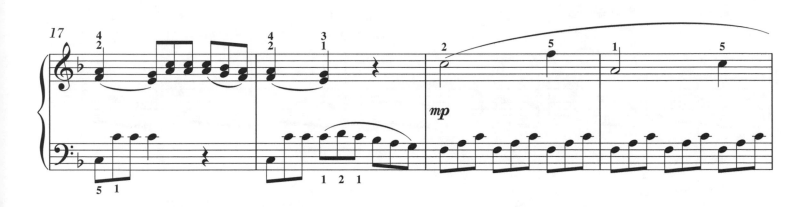

42

III

ABOUT THE EDITOR

RICHARD WALTERS

Richard Walters is a pianist, composer, and editor of hundred of publications in a long music publishing career. He is Vice President of Classical Publications at Hal Leonard, and directs a variety of publications for piano, voice, and solo instruments. Walters directs all publishing in the Schirmer Performance Editions series. Among other piano publications, he is editor of the revised edition of *Samuel Barber: Complete Piano Music, Leonard Bernstein: Music for Piano*, and the multi-volume series *The World's Great Classical Music*. His editing credits for vocal publications include *Samuel Barber: 65 Songs, Benjamin Britten: Collected Songs, Benjamin Britten: Complete Folksong Arrangements, Leonard Bernstein: Art Songs and Arias, The Purcell Collection: Realizations by Benjamin Britten, Bernstein Theatre Songs, G. Schirmer Collection of American Art Song, 28 Italian Songs and Arias for the Seventeenth and Eighteenth Centuries*, 80 volumes of standard repertoire in the Vocal Library series, and the multi-volume *The Singer's Musical Theatre Anthology*. Walters has published dozens of various arrangements, particularly for voice and piano, and is the composer of nine song cycles. He was educated with a bachelor's degree in piano at Simpson College, where he studied piano with Robert Larsen and composition with Sven Lekberg, and graduate studies in composition at the University of Minnesota, where he studied with Dominick Argento.